MARVEL

ROCKET AND GROOT

THE HUNT FOR
STAR-LORD

WRITTEN BY
AMANDA DEIBERT

ILLUSTRATED BY
CAM KENDELL

SCHOLASTIC

First published by Scholastic in the US, 2023
This edition published by Scholastic in the UK, 2023
1 London Bridge, London, SE1 9BG
Scholastic Ireland, 89E Lagan Road, Dublin Industrial Estate, Glasnevin, Dublin, D11 HP5F

ISBN 978 0702 33305 7

13 5 7 9 10 8 6 4 2

Printed in the UK by Bell and Bain Ltd, Glasgow

First edition, September 2023
Artwork by Cam Kendell
Edited by Lori Wieczorek
Lettering by Taylor Esposito
Book design by Martha Maynard

MARVEL

Lauren Bisom, Senior Editor, Juvenile Publishing
Caitlin O'Connell, Associate Editor
Sven Larsen, VP Licensed Publishing
C.B. Cebulski, Editor in Chief

CHAPTER ONE

3

6

11

CREEAAK

UGH...

WE HAD HIM UNTIL THIS *RAT* PARKED A SHIP ON TOP OF US!

I AM *REALLY* GETTING SICK OF ALL THE DIGS AT MY APPEARANCE. FOR YOUR INFORMATION —

AHH! WATCH IT. STAR-LORD'S IN TROUBLE!

NEBULA, STAND DOWN.

THIS BETTER BE REAL, BECAUSE THANOS WAS JUST ABLE TO ESCAPE WITH A PLANET-KILLING DEVICE. YOU JUST ENDANGERED THE ENTIRE GALAXY.

I AM GROOT.

GROOT'S RIGHT — WE HAVE A BIGGER EMERGENCY RIGHT NOW. STAR-LORD'S BEING HELD FOR RANSOM, AND WE WERE HOPING YOU'D KNOW WHO TOOK HIM.

CHAPTER TWO

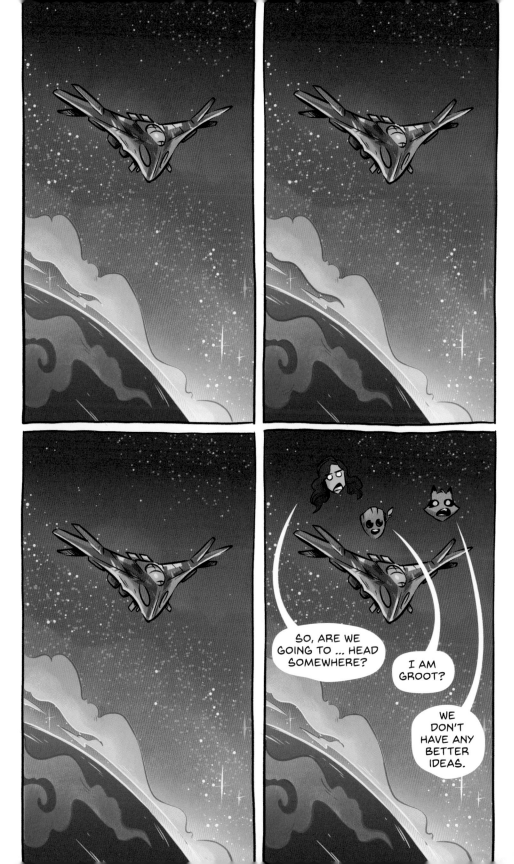

HA! HA! HA! HA!

HA! HA!

DID I SAY SOMETHING TO AMUSE YOU?

NAH, WE'VE JUST NEVER MET E.T.s BEFORE.

WHAT'S AN EEE-TEE?

APPARENTLY, THEY'RE GREEN LADIES, TALKING RACCOONS AND A TALKING TREE.

THIS IS GONNA BLOW UP MY FEED!

I AM GROOT.

UM, I AM CASS, AND THAT IS *MY PHONE!* I NEED IT BACK, LIKE, NOW.

IS THIS SAFE?

DEFINITELY NOT. SOCIAL MEDIA ENDED AT LEAST SEVEN OF MY FRIENDSHIPS.

DISARM IT.

EW, THE TECHNOLOGY IS SO ... OLD.

THAT PHONE IS *BRAND-NEW!* IT TOOK SO MUCH BABY-SITTING!

I TOO WAS FORCED TO SIT ON BABIES AS A GIRL.

WHAT?! LOGAN, WE NEED TO GO.

NOT UNTIL YOU TAKE US TO SEE DAVID HASSELON.

WE'LL TAKE YOU TO DAVID HASSELON, BUT YOU'LL HAVE TO DO A LITTLE SOMETHING FOR US FIRST.

SOME KINDA EARTH RITUAL?

YOU COULD SAY THAT. IT'S AN ANCIENT TRADITION WE CALL ...

23

WHEW! THAT MADE ME DIZZY. AND YOU'RE LOOKING A LITTLE GREEN TOO, GAMORA.

VERY FUNNY.

I AM GROOT?

I'M NOT SURE HE CAN HEAR YOU, BUDDY.

THAT DOESN'T MEAN THEY DON'T FEEL.

PAT PAT

YEAH, WE'RE VERY AWARE OF TREE EMOTIONS. YOU DO *NOT* WANNA SEE A GROOT GO THROUGH PUBERTY.

A WHAT?

I AM GROOT.

THERE IS **NO** PLANET B

WE BREATHE AS ONE

THIS IS *AMAZING!* SOMEONE GRAB THEIR PHONE, WE HAVE A SPOKES-TREE.

HEY!

I AM GROOT.

YEAH, WHAT HE SAID. NO MORE WEIRD RECTANGLES.

SNATCH

I GET IT. STAYING OFF THE GRID IS SMART PROTESTING. WE JUST WANT TO STOP DEFORESTATION.

THEY'RE TAKING AWAY YOUR FORESTS?

THERE'S NOT GOING TO BE ANY TREES LEFT.

THWACK

I AM GROOT!

CHAPTER THREE

I AM STILL TRACKING THANOS, BUT I HEARD NEWS THAT MAY HELP YOU.

WHAT IS IT, NEBULA?

I GOT WORD OF A PRISONER ON PLANET PANSNO.

THAT COULD BE ANYONE.

HE WAS LOCKED AWAY FOR ARROGANCE AND INSULTING THE LEADER OF THE PANSNOIAN RACE.

OHHH, HE GOT LOCKED UP FOR BEING A GENERAL JERK? YEAH, THAT'S STAR-LORD.

SEND US THE COORDINATES.

PANSNO

FANCY DIGS.

WE'VE COME TO, UH, REQUEST THE RELEASE OF YOUR PRISONER.

I AM GROOT.

RIGHT. TO *HUMBLY* REQUEST THE RELEASE OF YOUR PRISONER.

WHISPER WHISPER WHISPER

JUST BE READY FOR WHATEVER HAPPENS...

HERE ON PANSNO A GRIEVOUS INSULT MAY ONLY BE ATONED FOR IN ONE WAY.

AND WHAT MIGHT THAT BE?

A CHALLENGE OF COMBAT, OF COURSE.

IF YOU WOULD LIKE THE RELEASE OF YOUR FRIEND...

...THEN YOU MUST BE READY —

WE WERE BORN READY.

— TO ENGAGE IN A BATTLE OF ...

... DANCE!

DANCE?

PETER IS ON HIS OWN. HE LOVES TO DANCE. I DON'T KNOW WHY HE WOULDN'T HAVE JUST DONE IT HIMSELF.

WHEW, I ALMOST FORGOT WE WEREN'T ACTUALLY FIGHTING ANYONE.

ME TOO.

YOUR DANCE IS UNCONVENTIONAL. WE WILL BE SPEAKING OF IT FOR YEARS TO COME. YOU MAY HAVE YOUR PRISONER.

DRAX?!

AND SUDDENLY THE RUDENESS ALL MAKES SENSE. IT WASN'T STAR-LORD BRAGGING ABOUT BEING A GUARDIAN, IT WAS DRAX.

AH, MY FRIENDS. I HAVE TOLD THESE HIDEOUS BEINGS THEIR GRACE AND BEAUTY MAKE ME WANT TO VOMIT UNTIL MY EYES ARE FILLED WITH SO MUCH WATER I NO LONGER HAVE TO LOOK ON THEIR DISGUSTING VISAGE.

OF COURSE YOU DID.

CHAPTER FOUR

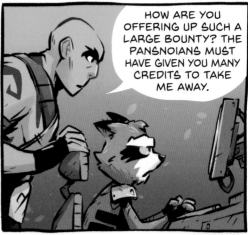

THE EASIEST WAY TO FIGURE OUT WHO IS HOLDING STAR-LORD FOR RANSOM IS TO OFFER AN EVEN BIGGER BOUNTY OURSELVES.

WE DON'T HAVE THE CREDITS FOR THAT.

I DIDN'T SAY WE'D ACTUALLY PAY. I HAVE A MUCH *BETTER* PLAN.

STAR-LORD
wanted : ALIVE
credits: 1,000,000,000,000

"FIRST, THE RAVAGER CLANS WILL TAKE THE BAIT.

"AND THEN ALL WE HAVE TO DO IS GET AHEAD OF THEM AT THE LAST MINUTE, SO WE DON'T HAVE TO PAY.

"IT'S A SIMPLE PLAN.

"WHAT COULD GO WRONG? IT'S TOTALLY EASY."

I AM GROOT!

DEATH'S HEAD! THINGS JUST GOT COMPLICATED.

DON'T BOTHER, IT'S TREE-PROOF, YES?

AND RAT-PROOF.

DON'T YOU HAVE BOUNTIES TO COLLECT?! WHY DID YOU GRAB *US*?!

NOT BOUNTIES. I AM A FREELANCE PEACEKEEPING AGENT, YES?

OH YEAH, I'M FEELING *REALLY* AT PEACE RIGHT NOW.

IT WILL BE PEACEFUL WHEN MY FEE IS PAID.

THERE IS NO ONE I HATE AS MUCH AS DEATH'S HEAD.

I AM GROOT?

OKAY, MAYBE THANOS, AND RONAN AND AYESHA AND HALA AND KNULL AND MOJO AND ...

... TASERFACE AND ULTRON SIGMA AND, OH, WHO WAS THAT GUY WHO PULLED MY TAIL WHEN WE WERE AT THAT LITTLE CAFÉ? I *HATE* THAT GUY ... WHAT WAS I TALKING ABOUT?

OOOFFFF!

WHAM

ZZZ!

YOU COULD HAVE GIVEN US A SMOOTHER LANDING!

TIME TO COLLECT.

I GUESS I SHOULD BE FLATTERED ANYONE IS OFFENDED ENOUGH TO OFFER MORE CREDS FOR US THAN FOR STAR-LORD. UNLESS YOU WERE JUST TOO *SCARED* TO COLLECT THAT ONE.

OUCH! OKAY, OKAY!

ZAP!

48

WHERE ARE WE GOING ANYWAY?

AS YOU REQUESTED.

THE ALETA RAVAGER CLAN?!

WHY HAVE ROCKET AND GROOT TAKEN UP OUR POST?

I DON'T THINK THAT'S WHAT HAPPENED.

LOOKS LIKE WE'RE GONNA NEED A NEW PLAN TO REPLACE ROCKET'S "GENIUS" PLAN.

I DO NOT THINK HIS PLAN WAS GENIUS. CLEARLY IT WAS VERY BAD.

FIRST, WE SAVE ROCKET AND GROOT. THEN WE FIND STAR-LORD. THEN WE SIT DOWN FOR A LESSON IN SARCASM.

THAT IS YOUR NEW PLAN? IT IS NOT VERY GOOD.

CHAPTER FIVE

ARE YOU TELLING ME YOU COULD HAVE DONE THIS THE WHOLE TIME?!

NO, STAR-LORD DOESN'T HAVE THE MASSIVE SIGNATURE OF THANOS'S CHAIR, *BUT...*

... I *CAN* TRACE THE ORIGIN OF THE ORIGINAL RANSOM BROADCAST.

WHY DID YOU NOT DO THAT IN THE FIRST PLACE?

BECAUSE *I DIDN'T* THINK OF IT, OKAY?! I DON'T SEE ANYONE ELSE COMING UP WITH BRILLIANT PLANS.

I SENSE MUCH ANGER HERE.

YOU ARE A MAN OF REFINED TASTE.

I'LL SHOW YOU REFINED TASTE!

WELL, THIS HAS BEEN FUN, BUT I HAVE A GALAXY TO CUSTODIAN.

I GUARANTEE I WAS HERE FIRST, SWORD GUY!

STAR-SWORD.

STAR-SWORD. SO HOW DID I EVEN GET — OH WAIT.

I GOT SOME PIZZA ON IT. YEP. IT DOES SAY, STAR-SWORD, CLEAR AS DAY.

I AM GROOT.

NEXT TIME, I CHECK THE RACCOON'S DATA PAD **BEFORE** WE GO ANYWHERE.

CREATOR BIOS

AMANDA DEIBERT IS A *NEW YORK TIMES* BESTSELLING COMIC BOOK AND TELEVISION WRITER. HER COMIC BOOK WRITING INCLUDES STAR WARS HYPERSPACE STORIES (LUCA FILM), DARKWING DUCK (DISNEY/DYNAMITE), DC SUPER HERO GIRLS, TEEN TITANS GO!, WONDER WOMAN '77, BATMAN AND SCOOBY DOO!, LOVE IS LOVE (*NYT* #1 BESTSELLER) AND MORE FOR DC COMICS, JOHN CARPENTER'S TALES FOR A HALLOWEENIGHT, VOLUMES 2-8 (STORM KING COMICS), AND MORE. HER TELEVISION WORK INCLUDES *HE-MAN AND THE MASTERS OF THE UNIVERSE* FOR NETFLIX AND FOUR YEARS AS A WRITER FOR FORMER VICE PRESIDENT AL GORE'S INTERNATIONAL CLIMATE BROADCAST, *24 HOURS OF REALITY*.

CAM KENDELL IS AN ILLUSTRATOR OF ALL THINGS WHIMSICAL AND/OR FANTASTICAL. HE HAS CREATED ART FOR BOOKS LIKE AARON REYNOLD'S SERIES FART QUEST, BOARD GAMES LIKE 5-MINUTE MYSTERY AND D&D'S DUNGEON MAYHEM, AND COMICS LIKE CHOOSE YOUR GNOME ADVENTURE AND FLOPNAR THE BUNBARIAN. WHEN NOT DRAWING GNOMES, CAM ENJOYS BIRDING, ROCKING ON THE ACCORDION, LOSING AT BOARD GAMES, AND HIKING IN THE BEAUTIFUL UTAH MOUNTAINS WITH HIS WIFE AND FOUR CHILDREN, HOPING TO SEE A BLACK BEAR... FROM A SAFE DISTANCE.

LOVED *ROCKET AND GROOT: THE HUNT FOR STAR-LORD?* TURN THE PAGE FOR A TEASER OF *SPIDER-HAM: HOLLYWOOD MAY-HAM!*

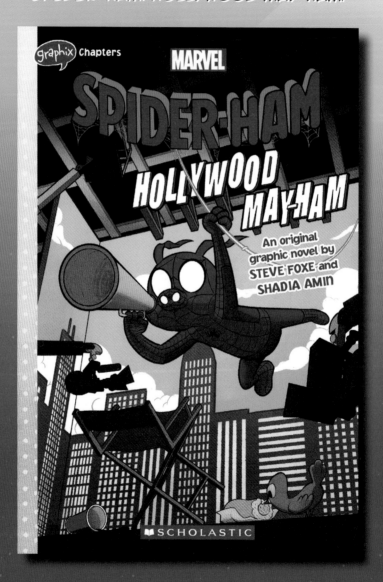

YOU'VE BEEN EXPOSED, MR. NEGATIGER!
SPIDER-HAM
• EVERYTHING YOU LOVE ABOUT SPIDER-MAN, IN CONVENIENT HAM FORM.
• WELL, ALMOST EVERYTHING.
Armstrong St

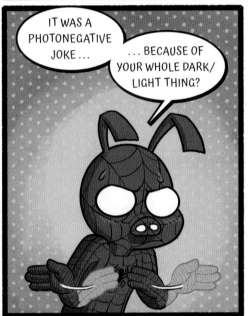